UNDERSTANDING THE SEASONS OF GOD

Dr. Joyce A. Louther

Copyright © 2007 by Dr. Joyce A. Louther

Understanding The Seasons Of God
by Dr. Joyce A. Louther

Printed in the United States of America

ISBN 978-1-60266-786-0

All rights reserved solely by the author. The author guarantees all contents are original and do not infringe upon the legal rights of any other person or work. No part of this book may be reproduced in any form without the permission of the author. The views expressed in this book are not necessarily those of the publisher.

Unless otherwise indicated, Bible quotations are taken from the New International Version of the Bible. Copyright © 1988, 1989, 1990, 1991 by Tyndale House Publishers, Inc., and the King James Version/Amplified Bible Parallel Edition, Copyright © 1995 by Zondervan.

www.xulonpress.com

Dedication

This book is dedicated to my lovely daughter Carlissa, born December 25, who is the best Christmas present God could have blessed me with.

To my father Louis, my mother Valerie, who went home to be with the Lord, my sister Louise, and my brother Quentin.

To Apostle Dr. John and Pastor Dr. Vickie Tetsola, my spiritual father and mother in the Lord.

To my Ecclesia Church International family.

Acknowledgments

To Apostle Dr. John Tetsola for first recognizing the scribe anointing.

To Elder Gregory Clark for his prophetic words of encouragement about my someday writing a book.

To Pastor Perry Mallory for his critique and direction.

A special thanks to Pastor Dr. Vickie Tetsola for her time, suggestions, support, insightful input, and encouragement.

Table of Contents

Introduction xi
Chapter I   The Seasons of God 15
Chapter II   The Season of Winter 19
Chapter III   The Season of Spring 33
Chapter IV   The Season of Summer 47
Chapter V   The Season of Fall 61
Chapter VI   Events in a Season 69
Chapter VII   Season of Barrenness 75
Chapter VIII   God's Faithfulness 81
Chapter IX   Principles to Understanding the
               Seasons of God 87
Chapter X   Conclusion 93

Introduction

In May 2001, I was privileged to deliver a Mother's Day message at my church. The message was simply titled "Seasons." When the service was over, a number of people thanked me and said they were blessed by the message. I felt a great sense of joy because in that brief time, God used me to shed insight on some questions people had about the seasons of God. Since then, while reading the Bible in my quiet time I could see where particular passages about certain individuals could apply to various spiritual seasons in life. This book is the outcome.

In general, a season is a period of time which can be applied to nature and to our lives. God in His infinite wisdom has punctuated all of life with seasons. As punctuation marks in written communication add meaning, variety, and clarity which causes the reader to pause for understanding, speed up with excitement, or end at the conclusion, so too do seasons punctuate life, adding emphasis and bringing meaning, variety, and clarity.

First, I would like to say not all seasons are experienced in every part of the world, so some people may have difficulty comprehending certain seasons. For example, people who have never seen snow might find it difficult to understand winter because they are in a tropical climate where it is warm all year round; others may not understand a hot summer day because they live in a subarctic climate where it is cold almost all year round. The same is true in individual lives. Some people have had relatively happy lives, while others have experienced a lot of heartache. I think the majority of us have experienced different intensities of each season throughout our lives, so it is important for the purpose of this book to discuss all the seasons.

In nature there is a natural progression of the seasons from winter to spring to summer to fall. There are laws of nature which must be followed that govern each season. In our lives, there are also seasonal changes, but these are spiritual seasons which are not governed by time, as we understand it. Like the laws of nature, there are laws of God which govern spiritual seasons that also must be followed. As surely as the seasons direct the course of nature, spiritual seasons direct the course of our lives.

One important point I need to emphasize is that we must be careful not to put God in a box. I use the sequence of natural seasons as a framework or a point of reference so the reader and I can be on the same page. We cannot assume that the progression from one spiritual season to another will be in any specific order.

Throughout this book, in various examples, I refer to seeds as the Word of God, and the heart as soil. The basis for this can be found in the following Scriptures:

> A sower went out to sow his seed...
> Luke 8: 5 (KJV)

> Now the parable is this: The seed is the word of God.
> Luke 8: 11 (KJV)

> ...And taketh away the word out of their hearts...
> Luke 8:12 (KJV)

We can see that the seed sown is the Word of God and the ground in which it is sown is the hearts of men. Man's heart, like soil, is capable of improvement and bearing fruit. As it is with soil, some hearts may take more work and preparation than others. We will also see the importance and significance of being obedient to the laws governing each season. Understanding and accepting the seasons of God and the changes that occur will bring peace, contentment, and security to our lives.

Chapter I

The Seasons of God

As the earth circles around the sun, the believer's life circles around the Son of God. Like the earth, we will all experience different seasons in our lives. Seasons are powerful forces that can affect the activities we do, the foods we eat, the clothes we wear, and even the mood we are in. The key to advancing from one spiritual season to the next is the ability to understand what season we are in and how to properly respond while we are in it.

Seasons Are God's idea

> As long as the earth endures, seedtime and harvest, cold and heat, summer and winter, day and night will never cease.
>
> Genesis 8:22

Because of man's sinfulness, God flooded the earth to destroy all life. Only Noah, his family, and the animals on the ark were saved. God promised never to flood the earth again, and He established the seasons with their changes as a constant reminder of this.

What Is a Season?

By definition, a season is any one of the four divisions of the year, as defined by the position of the Earth in its orbit around the sun. The four seasons, winter, spring, summer, and fall, are characterized by differences in temperature and differences in the length of daylight. A season can also be described as a period of special activity, as we read in Ecclesiastes 3:1: "There is a time for everything, and a season for every activity under the heaven."

Seasons are an integral part of God's program for the earth and for His people. Just as there are seasons in nature, the physical body, and life, there are also spiritual seasons.

What Are the Characteristics of a Spiritual Season?

There are a number of things we must keep in mind. First, spiritual seasons are not locked into a timeframe like natural seasons. We cannot set a specific length of time for any given season using days, weeks, months, or even years. Second, changes in a season or the change from season to season can be gradual or sudden. How do we know when we are moving into a new season? We know we are moving into a new season when we see, sense, feel, or discern that our circumstances have changed or are changing. Third, a season can be seen as a period of activity; and within the activity there are specialized actions that need to occur. Sometimes an activity is limited to a particular season and there are actions that are limited to a specific activity.

Preparation for the Coming Season

In nature there is work that must be done in each season, and the amount of labor and toil will depend on the season. That is, one season may require more work than another. To do the required work, there are tools that are needed. This is also true for spiritual seasons. We will need to know what the tools are, how to use them, when to use them, and in which season to use them. We must also be aware of any danger, difficulties, or hardships which are related to the various seasons. There are warning signs in each season, and we need to know what they are and how we can protect ourselves.

The natural seasons are divided into four segments—winter, spring, summer, and fall. I'll use these same divisions as a reference as we look at the spiritual seasons in life. Did you ever notice that when you talk about seasons, you list them in a certain order? Typically, we say, "Winter, spring, summer, and fall." It seems almost like an ingrained speech pattern. Since this order seems to be the natural progression, we will look at winter first.

Chapter II

The Season of Winter

What is winter? In North America, winter is the coldest season of the year, extending from the end of autumn to the beginning of spring. It is a time characterized by the lack of life, warmth, and cheer. By this definition, we find the very first winter in the Bible in the book of Genesis:

> Now the earth was formless and empty, darkness was over the surface of the deep…
> Genesis 1:2a

But all is not hopeless. As we keep reading, we see the verse continues with "and the Spirit of God was hovering over the waters." What does this mean? It reveals to us that even in our deepest, darkest winter, God is with us, hovering at the edge, waiting to enter in.

Winter is a season that does not lend itself to much activity. The amount of activity sometimes depends on us—how we interact with our environment or react to our circumstances. As we look at our spiritual lives, we may get frustrated with what we perceive to be a lack of activity. For instance, you may be standing on a promise of God or you may have received a prophetic word from the Lord, but you don't see anything happening, you don't see the manifestation, everything looks dark, and there does not appear to be any life. You are in a winter season. There are a number of things you can do. You can spend your time on the computer, surfing the Internet, visiting chat rooms, and playing videogames. Or you can sit in front of the television, channel surfing with the remote. Or you can spend your time complaining about your situation, crying, "Why, God, why? "or "When, God, when?" However, the best way you can spend this time is by getting closer to God. This is accomplished through studying, reading, and meditating on His Word and promises as He hovers over your winter.

Winter can wreak havoc with you physically, mentally, emotionally, and spiritually. It can break your focus, take you away from the things of God, and take your mind off God. You will begin to focus on yourself, saying, "I feel tired, I feel depressed, I feel afraid, I feel lonely." Everything is "I, I, I." We focus only on our immediate needs and wants. We have to turn our focus to the only source of help. We must read and meditate on the Word of God, hiding the seed of the Word in our hearts, using the Word to protect us from the attacks of Satan. We must realize there may not be any outward signs of change, and even though the time seems cold, dark, and lifeless, the Holy Spirit is busy at work on the inside of us. We must understand that we have to operate in faith, walk in obedience, and not give up hope in order to survive this season.

Going back to nature, seeds of all common tree fruits such as apple, pear, peach, and cherry go through a dormant period before they germinate and produce new plants. *Dormant* means "to be inactive or sleeping." This is part of the natural cycle; a cycle is a period of time. We can see this same process in the lives of the people of God. We can look at this dormant period as silent years where God is building and preparing us in private for our public promotion. In Scripture, there are examples of men of God who faced their own private winter and survived:

1. Abraham waited almost twenty-five years before the birth of his child of promise (Genesis 15 and 21).
2. Joseph experienced almost fourteen years of slavery and imprisonment before seeing the reality of his dream (Genesis 37-45).
3. Moses spent almost forty years in the desert before carrying out the call of God as the deliverer of Israel (Exodus 2:11-5:1).

During the years of waiting, it may seem as though nothing is happening. Spiritually we can feel stripped bare, buried in isolation and forgotten. We all want to be and feel productive, inventive, and creative. But because of inactivity we may feel useless, like we're wasting time, spinning our wheels, and going nowhere fast. We must remember that production is only one part of a cycle in the season and it is always preceded by a dormant period.

It is important for us to realize that we must protect ourselves spiritually during winter in the same way we protect ourselves naturally in this season. We must be aware that everyone does not survive the winter in the natural or in the spiritual realm. We must be alert to the dangers we can encounter and try to avoid them.

Dangers in the Winter Season

In the natural, if you are caught outside in extremely cold weather, one of the dangers is frostbite. Frostbite occurs when certain parts of the body become frozen, such as the ears, fingers, and toes. This can happen because the person is not properly dressed or insulated. If not treated in time, these parts will become gangrenous and die. Gangrene is the death of a body part caused by a lack of adequate blood supply, and the dead part has to be amputated. *Amputate* means "to cut off or sever." How does this relate to us spiritually? There are various areas of function and ministry we do in the spiritual realm. And, like parts of the body, these functions can become frozen and die due to lack of spiritual use. Examples are prayer and faith. Prayer changes things and faith can move mountains. Both are spiritual forces that will become ineffective if not used or exercised. We can hinder or limit the movement of the Holy Spirit in our lives through neglect. We can lose precious ground in these and other specific areas of our spiritual walk to the point where it is possible to never regain or recover the same momentum or pursuit.

Another danger of being caught in the cold weather is death of the physical body. I'm not talking about being caught out in some remote area. This can happen in the city, even with plenty of food and shelter around. For whatever reason, some people get separated from their source of food and shelter, exposing themselves to the elements of nature. Typically, exposure to the cold decreases the blood circulation in the body, so the brain does not get enough oxygen. This happens so slowly that the person doesn't realize they're dying; they feel very tired and just want to lie down and go to sleep. But once they go to sleep, if they are not rescued in time, they never wake up.

The same thing can happen to us spiritually if we don't stay active in the things of God during this season. We must keep our spiritual circulation going by not letting it slow down. How can this be accomplished? We start by renewing and affirming our faith in God. Next, we renew our minds with the Word of God. Then we renew our commitment to the things of God. We continue the strengthening process by coming out to services in the local church, staying in prayer and intercession, fasting, studying and meditating on the Word of God, participating and functioning in the ministry of helps. It is of the utmost importance to keep covered; this means we must be planted in a local church. Being planted in a local church will help protect us from the attacks of the enemy. The local church is the source of food and shelter for the spirit. This is where we connect with the man or woman of God, the one who holds the key to our destiny. We must choose to follow our pastor as he or she follows Christ. As the pastor is commanded to feed the sheep, we must be willing to eat.

It is extremely important not to murmur or complain about our situation or circumstances. There is a subtle difference between murmuring and complaining. For the purpose of this book, to murmur is a half-repressed utterance, basically it is speaking to oneself; to complain is by speech, something said aloud for others to hear. Murmuring and complaining reveals a defect in the heart and can harden it.

Winter can be a time of sickness, disappointment, or rejection; these are clearly major issues. But sometimes even small annoyances will let us know we are in a winter season. You may be in good health, be financially stable, and still experience difficulties. Your timing seems to be off; decisions you make don't seem work out; and no matter what you do, you feel "out of sorts." This can be an indication that you are in a winter season. There are some who will experience a severe winter and some a mild one. Either way, we must keep our focus on God and be mindful that every bleak winter carries with it the promise of spring.

We will look at examples of men who did not survive their winter season; the first is Gehazi.

Gehazi

Gehazi, the servant of Elisha the man of God, said to himself, "My master was too easy on Naaman, this Aramean, by not accepting from him what he brought. As surely as the Lord lives, I will run after him and get something from him.

2 Kings 5:20

First, I want to take a brief look at Elisha. There was a time when Elisha had been a faithful servant to the prophet Elijah; this was Elisha's winter season. When it was time for Elijah to leave the scene, his mantle was passed to Elisha. We can view this as the model for Gehazi's promotion. At this time Gehazi, the servant to Elisha, was in the background. This was his winter season. Although he was in the background, Gehazi was able to assist in some of his master's miracles. It was Gehazi who suggested that the childless Shunammite woman be granted a son. Later, when the son became ill, Gehazi was sent ahead to lay Elisha's staff on the child.

Up to this time, Gehazi was a helpful, dedicated servant to Elisha. Gehazi was probably getting his "salary" so to speak from Elisha. Gehazi may have gotten "paid" at those times Elisha decided to accept gifts.

> ... Is it a time to receive money, and to receive garments, and oliveyards, and vineyards, and sheep, and oxen, and menservants, and maidservants?
>
> 2 Kings 5:26b (KJV)

Gehazi may have felt it was time for a raise or at least a bonus. But he could not wait. He decided to get the money on his own, and this proved to be his downfall. Gehazi saw what he thought was a perfect opportunity to line his pockets by asking Naaman for the reward Elisha had refused.

> Everything is all right," Gehazi answered. "My master sent me to say, "Two young men from the company of the prophets have just come from the hill country of Ephraim. Please give them a talent of silver and two sets of clothing."
>
> 2 Kings 5: 22

We can see at least four major problems with Gehazi: First, he asked for and accepted money that had been offered to someone else. Second, he implied that the money was in exchange for God's free gift of healing. Third, Gehazi lied by trying to cover up his meeting with Naaman, and fourth, he failed to mention the clothes and money he received.

> Then he went in and stood before his master Elisha. "Where have you been, Gehazi?"

Elisha asked. "Your servant didn't go anywhere," Gehazi answered.
2 Kings 5: 25

It seems Gehazi's desire for personal gain was more important than his service to God. He was not content in his position of servitude and could not wait to receive his reward from the Lord. He took it upon himself to ask for something that was not for him or offered to him. By coveting someone else's position and moving out of God's timing he became leprous.

Naaman's leprosy will cling to you and to your descendants forever." Then Gehazi went from Elisha's presence and he was leprous, as white as snow.
2 Kings 5: 27

Although he did not lose his life, he was disqualified for promotion, and we don't hear anything else about Gehazi's service in the Bible.

How This Relates to Believers

Well, there are individuals in the church today who are in trusted positions and serving faithfully. These individuals are very active in church; some are in a visible capacity while others may be behind the scene. At some point they begin to feel they are not getting paid their due or rewarded. The motive behind their ministry or assistance to ministry now becomes financial gain instead of service to the Lord. Some of these individuals decide they cannot wait. How do we know? We see increasing stories in the news media of a church bank account disappearing, or a building fund missing, or the mission's collection taking a walk, or an investment vanishing. Eventually, the person may be caught and prosecuted, but in reality they did not steal from man. They stole from God, and they will have to appear in His court. Although these people did not lose their lives, and some may even get the opportunity to return to the church or ministry, they have placed themselves in a position where it would be difficult to ever trust them again. They threw away their usefulness in the kingdom of God for a momentary monetary gain.

The next individual we will look at is Absalom.

Absalom

The story of Absalom is a complicated one, so I will focus on the period of time when he tried to over throw his father, King David:

> And there came a messenger to David, saying, The hearts of the men of Israel are after Absalom.
>
> 2 Samuel 15: 13 (KJV)

Absalom had been waiting to come into his inheritance, the throne of Israel. This was his winter season. However, due to his past history with his father, King David, Absalom began to feel he could do a better job. Although his ascension to the throne was uncontested, his hatred for his father caused him to take matters into his own hands. Absalom used his winning personality and good looks in a methodical campaign to build a loyal following for himself and stir up resentment against David. A battle ensued and Absalom was killed. Absalom could not wait to inherit the throne and died in the process of trying to get it illegally.

How This Relates to Believers

There are men and women of God today who have invested in and mentored spiritual sons and daughters. These are individuals into whom they have been imparting wisdom and knowledge, someone who could take the reins of leadership. Ascension or promotion to the position would be uncontested. But the person decides not to wait. He or she feels they can do a better job and now is the time. As far as they're concerned, the leader and mentor can teach them nothing else.

This has been one of the major causes of church splits. Unknown to the pastor, the son or daughter becomes distant because of some offense and begins to quietly build up a following through deception and manipulation. Instead of seeking to establish their own congregation, they try to steal a ready-made one. When the person is confident he or she has enough people and backing, they will announce their readiness to replace the senior pastor. He or she is now God's mouthpiece and is the one with the vision. This puts the members in a position to have to choose who they will follow. The biblically sound members will stay with the senior pastor. The son or daughter and the newfound congregation will try to make it on their own, but they will be doomed to fail. By moving out before God's timing and trying to usurp the pulpit, the person has put himself in a deadly position because God will not anoint or bless unfaithfulness, disloyalty, or disobedience.

This same quest for self-promotion can also be seen in the workplace. While waiting for a promotion, people can feel frustrated and discontented. They might begin to criticize and find fault with the boss. People will often use backstabbing, manipulation, and office politics to get ahead. This is not only true of nonbelievers. but believers as well. This reveals how self-centered instead of God-centered we can be. It shows our unbelief in the wisdom of God and our lack of faith in the competence and goodness of God. It also reveals our lack of patience, because when we look at the Word of God, it says, "But let patience have her perfect work, that ye may be perfect and entire, wanting nothing" (James 1:4, KJV).

We can also mediate on Philippians 1:6 (KJV): "Being confident of this very thing, that he which hath begun a good work in you will perform it until the day of Jesus Christ."

When we understand our spiritual winter season, we will not become angry, bitter, or resentful with God. We must know that God loves us and going through this season is not a punishment, but an opportunity to develop a deeper relationship with

Him. We must be content in our winter season and keep in mind that the next season can be upon us as suddenly as when God said, "Let there be light" in Genesis 1:3 (KJV).

Chapter III

The Season of Spring

What is the spring season? Spring in some areas is the season in which vegetation starts anew, the weather is warmer, and the days are longer. It is also a time of increased activity and preparation. The agricultural activities in this season include plowing and sowing. In our spiritual lives, each one of us will also experience times of plowing and sowing. Every activity in this season should be experienced in full with all its challenges and pleasures.

Activities in the Spring Season

In the natural realm, the growth process starts with the planting of a seed. But before planting, we must talk about the soil. Soil is the loose material that covers the land surfaces of the earth and supports the growth of plants. Our hearts are referred to as soil in the Bible, and this soil also supports seed (the Word of God) for growth. We will look at soil management and apply these principles to our lives. One of the practices in soil management is tillage. Tillage is the first step in the process of soil management. Tillage is putting and keeping soil in order for the production of crops, as through plowing, harrowing, hoeing, and sowing. We'll take a closer look at each activity and the tools needed.

The first step in tillage is plowing, and the tool used is called a plow. A plow is an implement for cutting, turning over, stirring, or breaking up the soil. *Plowing* is defined as: "to turn a surface of land with a plow; to turn up soil with a plow; to advance laboriously, plod." So the question is: Why do our hearts need to be plowed? Like the farmer who has to break up the soil to prepare it for seed, our hearts must also be broken up to prepare them to receive seed, which is the Word of God. We all have some area of resistance toward God or the things of God. For each person it is different, but these areas must be worked on. At times the task seems too hard; you may feel you're just plodding along. You may have been trying to change some area in your life and you get the feeling you will never change, but nothing is impossible for God. Once the plowing is done, you feel a sense of relief and you think you can sit back and relax, only to find there is more work to do. This is because during the plowing process, clods were formed. Clods are lumps of earth which can hinder seed growth. This means further refining of the soil must be done before seeds can be planted. The same applies to our hearts. This is not an easy task, but we must cooperate with the dealings of God no matter how painful, and move on to the next step to get rid of the clods.

The second step in tillage is harrowing, and the tool used is the harrow. The harrow is a farm implement that usually has a frame set with spikes, teeth, or disks. Harrowing is the process of leveling plowed ground and breaking clods. Rollers with v-shaped wheels break up clods of soil to improve the aeration of the soil and its capacity for absorbing water. As we apply this activity to our hearts, like the soil, clods have to be broken up into smaller pieces. We can look at clods as specific areas in our lives that we must contend with. These areas will vary for each individual. For example, have you heard a message about tithing, but you are not tithing consistently? Or have you heard a message regarding forgiveness, but there are times you still harbor resentment? These are areas that must be submitted to this process, otherwise we could stunt our spiritual growth. Once harrowing is finished and the clods have been broken up, we think we can take a break, but there is still more work to be done. No matter how tired we feel or uncomfortable we get, we should not try to rush or bypass any part of these processes.

The third step in tillage is hoeing, and the tool used is the hoe. A hoe is used for loosening the earth or digging up weeds. Let's take a closer look at the weed. Weeds are unsightly and troublesome plants that grow in abundance with little or no nurturing. The term "weed" actually applies to any plant that grows where it is not wanted. It is usually characterized by rapid growth and typically replaces other, more desirable plants. There are a number of ways to remove weeds, from simply pulling them out by hand, to hoeing, to using elaborate chemical weed killers. With any method, the best time to deal with weeds is when they are young and the roots are shallow. If we procrastinate, the weed will develop deep taproots. The taproot is the principle descending root of any plant, so the plant will grow back again if the taproot is not completely destroyed. This means we will have to weed again and again.

In the spiritual realm, weeds represent sin in the life of a believer or those areas that have not been turned over or submitted to God. In the believer's life, sin, like weeds can spring up at any time and tempt us to take our attention away from the things of God or to do things independent of Him. Some of the weeds that could manifest in our lives are doubt, unbelief, anger, bitterness, jealousy, envy, and offense, which replace the fruit of love, joy, peace, faith, patience, gentleness, and goodness. If we don't get to the root of the problem, it can become a besetting sin. Like the weed, it will continue to come back again and again, making life difficult, causing problems, and hindering our growth.

Most agricultural tools are kept in barns or storage sheds. For the spirit, the Bible contains all the tools needed to till the soil of our hearts. We must remember that no matter how painful or how long the process may take, it is necessary to submit ourselves to it if we are to mature and be ready for what God has prepared for us.

Planting Versus Sowing

Now that the soil has been prepared, we can either plant or sow seeds. Let's look at the difference between the two. *Planting* is defined as: "To set in the ground for growing; to furnish with plants or seed; to set in place firmly, put in position; to found, establish." *Sowing* is defined as: "To scatter (seed) over the land for growth."

In pondering the difference between planting and sowing, two ministry gifts come to mind: the pastor and the evangelist. The local church pastor plants seeds (sets seed in the ground) and the evangelist sows seeds (scatters seed for growth). A pastor is primarily responsible for the local church. He will invest in each congregational member, imparting and preparing him or her for ministry or assignment. The evangelist usually has a meeting where many people are gathered. He will impart into their lives and the people then go their own way. Some who have never attended a church will begin to attend, and those already in a church will have an increased level of commitment. Both men of God have imparted seeds for growth—one by planting, one by sowing.

The Growth Process

The next phase of the process is growth. *Growing* is defined as: "To increase in size by the assimilation of nutriment, progress toward maturity; to sprout and develop to maturity, as from a seed or spore; to flourish, thrive; to become more in size, quantity or degree; to become, come gradually; to cause to grow, raise by cultivation."

Let's take a closer look at the growth process. Once a seed is in the ground, the growth process begins. The growth process starts with budding. Budding occurs when a small part of the plant has begun to protrude through the soil. This brings expectancy and anticipation. The next step in the growth process is blossoming, which brings the expectancy into recognition. We call this the manifestation. Let's use the flower as an example. The manifestation is that time when we can see the shape and color, smell the fragrance, and touch the flower. As with the flower, we can see the promise of God or the prophetic word spoken over our lives begin to come into reality.

The next stage of growth is a time of fruit bearing. This part of the work is for preserving and sharing. Fruit bearing is rewarded with the repetition of the process. As we apply this principle to our spiritual lives, our fruit multiplies and progresses to a bountiful harvest. Let's look at how this fruit is manifested in our lives.

Manifesting Fruit

This fruit is manifested in our lives as the fruit of the Spirit. Galatians 5:22-23 (KJV) says, "But the fruit of the Spirit is love, joy, peace, longsuffering, gentleness, goodness, faith, meekness, temperance:

against such there is no law." The appearance of this fruit is the manifestation of the spontaneous work of the Holy Spirit in us as we yield ourselves to Him.

This fruit can also be manifested in our lives as prosperity. Psalm 1:3 (KJV) says, "And he shall be like a tree planted by the rivers of water, That bringeth forth his fruit in his season; His leaf also shall not wither; And whatsoever he doeth shall prosper." This is someone who, in the proper season and at the right time, will be loaded with fruit. Timeliness is extremely important; the fruit does not fall to the ground before it is ripe, nor does it hang on after maturity. This is a healthy, abundant crop.

And last, this fruit can be manifested in our lives in righteousness. Proverbs 11:30 (KJV) says, "The fruit of the righteous is a tree of life; and he that winneth souls is wise." This is a person whose life is a model for others, and it's the fruit of his tree that attracts people. This individual attracts others to lead them to Christ.

Although the growth process is the same for every believer, the rate of growth depends on what has been planted inside of us by God. We should try not to abnormally accelerate, slow down, take a shortcut, or bypass this process. We must master the foundations in order to see steady growth in our lives:

> Therefore leaving the principles of the doctrine of Christ, let us go on unto perfection; not laying again the foundation of repentance from dead works, and of faith toward God, Of the doctrine of baptisms, and of laying on

of hands, and of resurrection of the dead, and of eternal judgment.
Hebrews 6:1-2 (KJV)

As we grow and mature in these areas, other areas will be revealed to us.

The Need for Protection

There is another critical aspect of the work we need to discuss regarding this season, and that is the need for protection. *Protecting* is "to shield or defend from attack, harm, or injury; to guard or defend." The farmer may use a fence or insecticides. In the spiritual realm, this is accomplished by being planted in the house of God, the local church. This is our covering, our protection. This is the place where we can be nurtured, which will allow us to flourish and grow. We must also know how to use the Word of God to shield us from the attacks of the enemy (Satan), which could cause hurt, harm, or injury.

We will look at an example of a man of God who made it into the spring season but did not survive.

King David

> In the spring, at the time when kings go off to war David sent Joab out with the king's men and the whole Israelite army. They destroyed the Ammonites and besieged Rabbah. But David remained in Jerusalem.
> 2 Samuel 11:1

Why is this a spring season for David? David was in a season where the activity was to prepare for and go to war. He was supposed to get busy. Winter had passed. Winter in Israel was the rainy season, and it was the time when crops were planted. By spring, the wheat and barley were ready to be harvested. These crops were important because it was the main food source for traveling armies. Also, the dry roads made it easier for the troops, supply wagons, and chariots to move. Everyone and everything was ready and prepared for war, except David. Instead of going to battle, he went to bed. Let's look at what happened when David was not obedient to the work he was called to do in this season:

> One evening David got up from his bed and walked around on the roof of the palace. From the roof he saw a woman bathing. The woman was very beautiful.
> 2 Samuel 11:2

In staying home from war, David abandoned his purpose. Now he was idle and had time on his hands. In his idleness, he was taking a stroll, and someone caught his attention and kindled a desire in him. Now there is nothing wrong with desire when it is properly focused. A desire can be godly or ungodly. *Desire* is defined as: "to wish or long for; covet, crave; to express a wish for, ask for; or request." These are just a few of the many scriptures regarding godly desire:

> Brethren, my heart's desire and prayer to God for Israel is, that they might be saved.
> Romans 10:1 (KJV)

> Follow after charity, and desire spiritual gifts…
> 1 Corinthians 14:1a (KJV)

> This is a true saying, If a man desire the office of a bishop, he desireth a good work.
> 1 Timothy 3:1 (KJV)

> As newborn babes, desire the sincere milk of the word, that ye may grow thereby:
> 1 Peter 2:2 (KJV)

But the focus of David's desire was toward the wrong person.

> Neither shalt thou desire thy neighbour's wife, neither shalt thou covet thy neighbour's house, his field, or his manservant, or his maidservant, his ox, or his ass, or any thing that is thy neighbour's.
> Deuteronomy 5:21 (KJV)

Temptation came, and David gazed at it instead of running away from it. Not only did he sin, but he sinned deliberately.

The woman conceived and sent word to David, saying, "I am pregnant."
2 Samuel 11:5

David knew what he did was wrong and attempted to conceal his sin. First, David tried to manipulate Uriah, Bathsheba's husband, so he would go home and view the child as his, but that did not work. Then David tried another tactic; he thought he could cover his tracks by having Uriah set up and killed in the war. This appeared to be successful. David felt safe, but he could not hide what he did from God. God in His infinite mercy and grace waited for David to repent. But David thought he had gotten away with murder, and repentance was the last thing on his mind. Almost a year had gone by before David was confronted by God, but he still had to pay the price for his sin. Sometimes we think we can sin and cover it up, but we must remember that the more we try to cover our sin, the more we become insensitive toward what we are doing and eventually view it as right.

How This Relates to Believers

This can be compared to people in the church who decide they want to take a break, slow down, take it easy, or cut back on ministry activities or duties. There is nothing wrong with this if that is what God is leading you to do. However, if it is your idea to do this, then it is a very dangerous place to be in. While wandering aimlessly throughout your day without focus and purpose, you can come into contact with someone or something you would normally have avoided. You begin to entertain wrong thoughts, participate in wrong activities, or get involved in the wrong relationships. Any of these distractions can lead to walking into sin. Notice I said walking, not falling, because this is a deliberate, conscious decision. However, once you acknowledge the wrong, you can immediately ask for forgiveness, but you must accept the consequences for your action. Don't do as David did; don't wait to be confronted by God.

What to Do When Tempted

What can we do to help ourselves when we are tempted away from what God has called us to do in our spring season?

1. We must go to God in prayer and seek His guidance regarding people, places, situations, and things that may tempt us.
2. We can memorize and meditate on Scriptures, especially those that speak to our specific area of weakness.
3. We should not isolate ourselves. We need to find another believer with whom we can share our struggles and be accountable to.
4. We can do as Job did in Job 31:1 (KJV): "I made a covenant with mine eyes; why then should I think upon a maid?" I believe this Scripture speaks to both men and women. Although we are aware we should not daydream, ponder, meditate, or physi-

cally study the opposite sex, we should make a conscious effort to be careful of other media we look at. Sometimes that can be difficult since certain media are very abundant in some cultures. Whether it is television, movies, videos, DVDs, books, magazines, newspapers, or catalogs, we must be selective in what we view. We also need to be just as careful of the websites we visit on the computer. The bottom line: do not look at anyone or anything ungodly that will cause you to be distracted. Keep your focus on God and what He has assigned you to do.

5. We must also know and believe 1 Corinthians 10:13: "No temptation has seized you except what is common to man. And God is faithful; He will not let you be tempted beyond what you can bear. But when you are tempted, He will also provide a way out so that you can stand under it."

One of the biggest lies the enemy uses against us when we're tempted is that no one else is going through what we're going through. This causes us to isolate ourselves and wallow in self-pity. We might even try to take matters into our own hands as David did. But God is telling us that we are not unique and we are not alone in our struggles. There is always a way of escape. God in His infinite wisdom, grace, and mercy gives us the ability to overcome. In any struggle, it is important to know when to run and when to fight. We will know what to do in any situation or circumstance when we listen to the voice of God; obey His Word; and receive the people He sends to help, support, encourage, and direct us.

Although we may like the activities we are doing in this season, we must understand this is preparation for the next season; we should not settle in and think there is no need for change.

How can we tell we're ready to move into the next season? Let's look at Luke 21:30 (AMP): "When they put forth their buds and come out in leaf, you see for yourselves and perceive and know that summer is already near."

Growing in this season will move us into the next season, which is summer.

Chapter IV

The Season of Summer

In New York, summer is the warmest season of the year. It is a fortunate, happy, and joyous season; a bright and prosperous period. It is the time for enjoying the beaches, parks, and zoos. In the natural realm, summer in a well-tended garden means abundance. Flowers are blooming, vines are growing up trellises, and vegetables are ripening. Summer is a time of harvesting. *Harvest* is defined as: "a crop, as of grain, gathered or ready for gathering; the time of gathering; the product of any toil or effort. It does not matter if it's flowers, fruits, or vegetables. Harvesting has to be done at the optimum stage of readiness.

The Harvest

Let's look at flowers for one example of harvesting. Listed below is a sample of how and when some flowers are harvested or gathered:

Alstroemeria is cut when the flowers begin to open; baby's breath is cut when half the flowers on the stem are open; China aster is cut when the flower is partially open; Chrysanthemums are cut when the flowers open; cockscomb is cut when it is at least seventy-five percent developed; Dutch irises are cut when the buds show color; hydrangeas are cut when the flowers have color.

It is extremely important that harvesting is done at the right time, because when done at the right time, it produces a long-lasting bouquet of flowers.

When we look at this spiritually, believers are at different stages of growth and development. Some are just budding and others are flowering. In our Christian walk we must be very careful not to compare ourselves with one another. Some individuals have a greater hunger for the things of God and mature faster spiritually. It does not matter how long you have been born again; someone coming to Christ after you may surpass you, so you must wait patiently and not become envious or jealous when someone else is blooming or receives a promotion. On the other hand, those who have been promoted must not become proud and haughty or look down on the ones who are still waiting. Our heavenly Father knows when it is our time to be harvested; only He knows when we are ready for that promotion or assignment. When it is our time of harvest, we will be able to walk in the full manifestation of our calling with ease. Waiting on God's timing is the only way to produce long-lasting results in our lives.

Another example we can look at are fruits; because there is also an optimal time for their harvest. We know that fruit harvested too soon will not ripen. In the spirit this is a sign of immaturity, someone who moved ahead of God's timing. If the fruit is harvested too late, the fruit will be overripe. Spiritually, this is someone who is full of the Word but has not moved out in God's timing either because fear or complacency; waiting too long produces someone who just warms the pew. Again, we see how important it is to obey God's timing.

Danger in the Summer Season

As wonderful as summer is, we can also perish in the summer. We can experience a time of drought. What is a drought? A *drought* is defined as: "long continued dry weather, want of water; scarcity; dearth (lack, famine); thirst."

> When the heaven is shut up, and there is no rain, because they have sinned against thee; yet if they pray toward this place, and confess thy name, and turn from their sin…
> 2 Chronicles 6:26 (KJV)

In the Bible, rain represents God's blessing, divine favor, and approval. A lack of rain would indicate the absence of His blessing. So even in a period of abundant prosperity, we could suddenly find ourselves in a drought or a state of not experiencing God's blessing and presence. We will look at examples of men who made it to the summer season but not survive.

Nadab and Abihu

> Moses and Aaron, Nadab, and Abihu, and the seventy elders of Israel went up and saw the God of Israel. Under his feet was something like a pavement made of sapphire, clear as the sky itself.
> Exodus 24:9-10

We see that Nadab and Abihu, two of Aaron's sons, had the privilege of experiencing a strong manifestation of the presence of God. As we continue to read, we see they are set aside for their assignment.

> Anoint them just as you anointed their father, so they may serve me as priests. Their anointing will be to a priesthood that will continue for all generations to come.
> Exodus 40:15

Aaron had four sons who were called to the ministry, but the two eldest, Nadab and Abihu, had been previously summoned by God and actually experienced the manifest presence of the Lord. They had just entered into their summer season; they were anointed for the priesthood. As we continue reading, we see disaster strikes:

> Aaron's sons Nadab and Abihu, took their censers, and put fire in them and added incense; and they offered unauthorized fire before the Lord, contrary to his command. So fire came out from the presence of the Lord, and consumed them, and they died before the Lord.
> Leviticus 10:1-2

What was the sin of Nadab and Abihu? Not only did they offer unauthorized fire before the Lord, but the offense was compounded by a series of breaks in protocol which led to their death. First, they were unauthorized to perform the incense service, the highest and most solemn service of the priestly office. Another break in protocol was that they decided to perform together a work that was the duty of one; they totally ignored the standard operating procedure. Another error is that they used fire that was not taken from the altar. And last but not least, they presumed to enter into the Holy of Holies, a place which only the high priest was to have access to.

Nadab and Abihu had just entered their summer season. They were set apart and consecrated for duty the day before. As part of their work as priests, they were to assist; only Moses and Aaron were to enter into the tabernacle. Nadab and Abihu felt they had "arrived" and they were so proud of the honor of their new advancement that while the people were still worshiping the Lord, they rushed to the tabernacle. They were more than eager to perform the highest, most honorable, and most visible part of the priestly work. But they were careless, irreverent, and out of God's timing. Their behavior aroused the divine displeasure of God, and they died in the very act of their sin. So even though they were recently anointed and promoted, their disobedience, carelessness, and irreverence cost them their lives. They suffered a drought and did not survive to enter into the next season.

How This Relates to Believers

In the church there are those who have come into their summer season, people who have been raised up and promoted to certain positions of authority in the church. They are called, appointed, anointed, and given the boundaries of their duties. This is how they, like Nadab and Abihu, can enter a drought in their summer season. A good example is what occurs when the pastor is away.

The pastor feels he can entrust the eldership he has raised up with the assignment of running the ministry while he is away. Two of the elders are assigned different aspects of the ministry to be in charge of. One is to minister the Word of God; the other is given administrative duties. However, they decide it's better to combine the assignment. The two get together and decide to make some changes. The flow of the house may be apostolic and prophetic; they decide it's time to emphasize evangelism, and the need for a better outreach such as a soup kitchen. They decide to change the order of the service being led by the flesh and not by the Holy Spirit; they also decide to take a special offering not authorized by the pastor. Do you think the man of God would ever leave these two in charge again? I don't think so! Upon his return, the pastor will have to clean up their mess; dispel any confusion and restore order. The pastor cannot strike them dead, but they can be demoted from their position and stripped of all authority in the ministry. This is a drought in their summer season and it's possible they may never attain their previous stature and positions.

Another example is King Saul.

King Saul

Therefore said I, The Philistines will come down now upon me to Gilgal, and I have not made supplication unto the Lord: I forced myself therefore, and offered a burnt offering.
1 Samuel 13:12 (KJV)

Saul had also entered into his summer season; he was now king. Saul was given a specific assignment and instructions. But before Saul was to start out on this particular assignment, Samuel was supposed to come and make an offering to the Lord. Samuel was to meet up with Saul within seven days. But when Samuel was late in arriving, Saul could not wait and decided to make the offering himself.

> And Samuel said to Saul, Thou hast done foolishly: thou hast not kept the commandment of the Lord thy God, which he commanded thee: for now would the Lord have established thy kingdom upon Israel forever. But now thy kingdom shall not continue: the Lord hath sought him a man after his own heart, and the Lord hath commanded him to be captain over his people, because thou hast not kept that which the Lord commanded thee.
>
> 1 Samuel 13:13, 14 (KJV)

Through his disobedience in trying to function in an office he was not called to, Saul lost the kingdom. Although Saul did not realize it, the loss was immediate in the spirit realm, but in the natural realm it was a gradual process. It was several years before the kingdom actually came under David's rule. Saul was not able to go to the next season.

How This Relates to Believers

What comes to my mind is a young minister in a congregation who feels he is called to be a pastor of a local church and also receives a word of the Lord that he will be a pastor. The senor pastor tells him he will be ordained before the people in the next church service. On the day of his ordination, the senior pastor is delayed, and the young minister is asked to minister the Word of God. The service begins. After prayer, praise, and worship, the senior pastor still has not arrived. The offering is taken, the psalmist sings, and still the senior pastor has not arrived. He completes the message, and looking at his watch, he wonders if there will be time for his ordination. He decides he will tell the people about his call and anoints himself. As soon as he's done, in walks the senior pastor. Because the young minister was out of order, this causes a drought in his summer season; his lack of character and impatience cost him his ordination, position, and standing.

Next we will look at Solomon, someone who experienced a drought late in his summer season.

King Solomon

> So king Solomon exceeded all the kings of the earth for riches and for wisdom.
> 1 Kings 10:23 (KJV)

Solomon was the greatest, most blessed person alive. As king, he was in his summer season.

> But king Solomon loved many strange women...
> 1 Kings 11:1-3 (KJV)

As great and wise as Solomon was, we see that even great wisdom and knowledge of God is not a defense against disobedience and idolatry. Solomon's falling away did not take place suddenly, but gradually, as he grew old. Although he continued to offer solemn sacrifices three times a year to the day of his death, his heart was no longer thoroughly devoted to the Lord, and he began to acknowledge the idols of his foreign wives and built them altars. No one had a better summer season than Solomon, yet he did not end well.

How This Relates to Believers

We can see this as someone in the church today who is well established in the things of God, blessed beyond measure. But the person makes wrong associations, and associations are extremely important, especially in marriage. This is someone who was in ministry, rooted and grounded in the Word, but got into a marriage not ordained by God, and soon after began to preach another gospel. The credibility is lost, and like Solomon, it started well, but did not end well.

We will look at two more examples of individuals who did not survive their summer season.

King Uzziah

> But when he was strong, his heart was lifted up to his destruction: for he transgressed against the LORD his God, and went into the temple of the LORD to burn incense upon the altar of incense. Then Uzziah was wroth, and had a censer in his hand to burn incense: and while he was wroth with the priests, the leprosy even rose up in his forehead before the priests in the house of the LORD, from beside the incense altar. And Uzziah the king was a leper unto the day of his death, and

dwelt in a several house being a leper; for he was cut off from the house, of the LORD: and Jotham his son was over the king's house, judging the people of the land.
2 Chronicles 26:16, 19, 21 (KJV)

Uzziah, as king of Judah, was in his summer season. After God gave him great prosperity and power, he became proud and tried to move out from the place God gave him. He became full of himself instead of remaining full of God. He tried to act like a priest and took a role that God did not anoint him to perform. He was so adamant about burning the incense that he did not stop even though the priests warned him. What got his attention was the appearance of leprosy on his skin in the middle of his raving. Uzziah was forcibly removed from the temple and remained leprous until his death. He declined in his summer season.

All the people previously mentioned were well known, but it does not matter what position, rank, station, or ministry you have because disaster can strike.

Amasa

And say to Amasa, Are you not my own and flesh and blood? May God deal with me, be it ever so severely, if from now on you are not the commander of my army in place of Joab.
2 Samuel 19:13

Usually when we look at this Scripture, the treachery of Joab is highlighted, but I want to look more closely at Amasa. Here is someone who found favor in the king's eyes and had been promoted. The king gave him a special task with specific instructions. He was disobedient by failing to keep within the timeframe he was allotted; he wound up in a place where he was not supposed to be, exposing himself to an unexpected enemy, which cost him his life. We see it is important not only to obey God, but to also obey those whom God has placed in authority over us, and follow God's timetable, not our own.

How This Relates to Believers

What does this mean for us today as we ponder the fates of King Saul, Nadab and Abihu, King Solomon, and King Uzziah? This is a warning that we must use the gifts, talents, abilities, and blessings God has given us in ways that please Him. We are never closer to failure than during our greatest success. If we fail to recognize God's part in our achievements, then these achievements are no better than failures.

In our summer season we must be aware of and avoid situations and people that will cause us to enter a drought. Being out of the presence of God is a place of drought, and we have examples that show us not everyone survived the drought. We must be very careful. In some instances we may never be able to enter into the presence of God again, as with Nadab and Abihu, King Saul, King Solomon, and King Uzziah. But today we have a better and new covenant. Disobedience does not mean the person has lost his or her salvation, for we can never be separated from the love of God, but our usefulness for the work of the kingdom and our fellowship with God is damaged.

This does not have to be the final outcome. We do not have to remain in a drought unless we want to. There is hope. As David was forgiven of his sin with Bathsheba, restoration is available to us.

We must understand this can be one of the most enjoyable seasons, but no matter what position God has called us to, God expects to be worshiped, honored, and obeyed. We must remember that everyone is subject to God's spiritual laws and consequences.

The next season we move into is fall.

Chapter V

The Season of Fall

Autumn is a time that is also referred to as fall. It is a time associated with maturity, but also with incipient decline. In the Midwest this is the time when the growing season winds down. The work for this season is watering, fertilizing, and removing old blooms. This is the time to kill any weeds that have blown into the soil. Spiritually, this is a time when we must examine our hearts, and if necessary, do as David did in Psalm 51:10 (KJV) and ask God "to create in us clean hearts and renew a right spirit within us." This is also the time for burning old plant growth. As Paul says in Philippians 3:13b (KJV), "... Forgetting those things which are behind…" In this season the leaf fall is the end of the cycle, but the leaf is perpetuated in the seasons to come with renewed growth.

So what is a leaf? A leaf is the part of the plant that serves primarily as the food-making organ. It is an extension of a plant's stem. Green leaves derive their color from a green pigment called chlorophyll; the presence of additional pigments causes other leaves to be red as in coleus or purple as in cabbage. In temperate regions of the world, the leaves of some plants change color in autumn. For example, leaves of garden plants turn yellow, but those of trees become a brilliant orange or red color. It is also interesting to note that in some plants, the leaves do not change color or fall off in autumn. Just as the leaf is the most prominent feature of the natural fall season, man is the most prominent feature in the spiritual season.

Since we don't live in a vacuum, we are often exposed to different atmospheres and environments. Because of this we sometimes pick up unwanted spiritual baggage. This is the season to take the time to examine and confirm what is in our hearts. There is a time for the leaf to fall naturally, but it can also fall unnaturally. As I mentioned previously, there are plants whose leaves do not change color or fall off in autumn. I'd like to compare Adam and Eve to the leaf that is not supposed to change color or fall off. Adam and Eve did not survive the fall season, and they fell away from the tree (God) instead of growing in God.

Adam and Eve

Adam and Eve were physically mature; however, they needed to develop spiritually. A test was given to them in the form of a command to not eat the fruit of a certain tree. Because they ate the forbidden fruit, their spiritual growth was interrupted. It is at this point that the "fall" began, and man started to slowly die (incipient decline). Since we also enter a fall season in our lives, we would not want to repeat the mistake of Adam and Eve.

Let's look at chapter three of Genesis:

> Now the serpent was more crafty than any of the wild animals the Lord God had made. He said to the woman, "Did God really say, You must not eat from any tree in the garden?" The woman said to the serpent, "We may eat fruit from the trees in the garden, but God did say, "You must not eat fruit from the tree that is not in the middle of the garden, and you must not touch it, or you will die." "You will not surely die." the serpent said to the woman. "For God knows that when you eat of it your eyes will be opened, and you will be like God, knowing good and evil."
>
> Genesis 3:1-5

Satan tempted Eve by getting her to doubt God's providence. Satan implied that there was a problem with God's word and gave Eve got the impression that God was holding out on her, that there was something He was not telling her. Satan played a simple game of misdirection, causing Eve to change her focus. She stopped looking at all God had given her and zeroed in on the one thing she could not have. Eve also misquoted God's Word. Let's look at chapter two of Genesis:

> But you must not eat from the tree of the knowledge of good and evil, for when you eat of it you will surely die.
>
> Genesis 2:17

The covenant was made with Adam and the mandate was given to him. Eve had not been taken out of Adam yet, so how did she know the fruit of this tree was forbidden? Adam, as the head, had the responsibility to tell her. However, we see she did not repeat the command correctly. She added they were not to touch the fruit. If you notice, Satan only talks about eating the fruit. Man was put in the garden to dress it and keep it. The two trees in the middle of the garden were not excluded from being cared for, but the fruit was excluded from being eaten. So when Eve touched the fruit after Satan's prompting and nothing happened, she began to meditate and ponder on it. Then she took it a step further and ate the fruit. But the fall, the breaking of the covenant itself, did not occur until Adam was disobedient and ate the fruit.

> ...She took some and ate it. She also gave some to her husband, who was with her, and he ate it. Then the eyes of both of them were opened...
>
> Genesis 3:6-7(KJV)

Eve was deceived, but Adam was not. He made a conscious decision to eat the fruit and disobey God. I've heard some say he did it because he was so in love with Eve. Another reason is maybe he realized that with Eve gone, he would be alone again.

> And Adam gave names to all cattle, and to the fowl of the air, and to every beast of the field; but for Adam there was not found an help meet for him.
> Genesis 2:20 (KJV)

Adam already knew what it was like to be alone, without companionship, without someone like himself. Even though he knew the command of God, he may have decided he could not live without her, and thus he decided to join her.

How This Relates to Believers

All believers have the same opportunity for growth and development in order to mature spiritually. We must know we are all fair game for Satan. He has not changed his style or his mode of operation. He still whispers in our ear, "Hath God said?" He still invites us to give in to his kind of lifestyle, a life of disobedience and separation from God. It is our choice to make if we decide to turn our backs on God's kind of life, a life of obedience and blessing.

> Know ye not, that to whom ye yield yourselves servants to obey, his servants ye are to whom ye obey; whether of sin unto death, or of obedience unto righteousness?
> Romans 6:16 (KJV)

The greatest tragedy is even though we have the Bible for reference and can see the outcome of disobedience: many still take Satan's bait. We are especially vulnerable if we have been believing God for something for a long time, standing on a promise, and waiting for a manifestation of His hand in our lives. The longer the wait, the more susceptible we are to listen to the question, "Hath God said?" This is why it is extremely important we are sure of what we believe and in whom we believe. We must not fall into the same trap of dwelling on what we don't have rather than on the countless blessings God has given us. Instead of feeling sorry for ourselves because of something that has yet to manifest in our lives, we must consider and be grateful for all we do have. We limit God when we take matters into our own hands. We must believe Him no matter what we think He can or cannot do in, for, and through our lives.

A Time for Reflection

For us, the work in this season of watering and fertilizing means to study and mediate on the Word of God so that, as it says in 2 Timothy 2:15, we can be workmen rightly dividing the word of truth.

The fall season can also be a time for reflection—to see where we have been, where we are, and where we are going. But this reflection must be kept in a proper perspective. We must be aware of the danger of self-exaltation in this season, which can lead to a rebellion against God. As soon as we take God out of our plans, we are placing ourselves above Him. We must not let anyone or anything take precedence over God in our lives. We must take this time to meditate on and thank God for His provisions, for enabling us to get this far.

Resisting Temptation

The key to surviving this season is resisting temptation. How do we resist temptation? First, we must realize that being tempted is not a sin. We have not sinned until we give in to the temptation.

The steps to resistance are simple:

- *pray* for strength to resist
- *say no* when confronted with what you know is wrong
- *run* from it.

James 1:12 (KJV) tells of the great blessings and rewards for those who don't give in when tempted: "Blessed is the man that endureth temptation: for when he is tried, he shall receive the crown of life, which the Lord hath promised to them that love him."

As fall season comes to an end, we must make sure we have prepared ourselves for the upcoming winter, as a new cycle will begin. There will be many seasons, and each season we effectively master with the tools provided will move us into the next level God has prepared for us.

Chapter VI

Events in a Season

The Bible is filled with various events that occur in the seasons. What is an event? An event is a happening, incident, or occurrence. Just as events occur in seasons, they also occur in the life of the believer. We can misinterpret the significance of these events if we don't understand them. Some of these events are:

Fruits Come in Due Season

> He is like a tree planted by streams of water, which yields its fruit in season and whose leaf does not wither. Whatever he does prospers.
> Psalm 1:3

Just as a tree soaks up water and bears luscious fruit, so must we soak up God's Word, producing proper actions and right attitudes that honor Him. We must faithfully follow God in order to flourish in the place where we have been planted or in the season in which we find ourselves.

Tears Come in a Season

> O my God, I cry out by day, but you do not answer, by night, and am not silent.
> Psalm 22:2

There are times in a season where we may experience something so traumatic that all we can do is cry out to God. At these times we may even feel abandoned by God. But the Word also says He will never leave us nor forsake us. We must hold on to this promise. We may also feel as if our prayers are not heard, but we must believe that God hears every cry although the answers to our prayer may be withheld or delayed.

And we are encouraged that "...weeping may remain for a night, but rejoicing comes in the morning" (Psalm 30:5b). When weeping comes, it is only to stay for an evening; singing will come in the morning. There is comfort in the fact that God is good and lets us know there is a limit to times of weeping.

These are two very powerful and comforting Scriptures. There are many things that may cause us to shed tears. And I believe everyone has shed tears of distress at some point in their lifetime. Depending on the personality, some cry more readily than others; it could be over a minor or catastrophic event. But the Word of God says that after the tears, we can expect a time of rejoicing.

Rainy Days Come in Seasons

In the natural realm, when most people think of rainy days, they usually think of gloom and dreariness. They think of it as interrupting their activity and plans. However, rain in the Bible is a symbol of God's blessing. God's Spirit is poured out to the believer as evidenced by the following verses:

> Then I will give you rain in due season, and the land shall yield her increase and the trees of the field shall yield their fruit.
> Leviticus 26:4 (KJV)

> Then I will send rain on your land in its season, both autumn and spring rains, so that you may gather in your grain, new wine and oil.
> Deuteronomy 11:14

> I will bless them and the places surrounding my hill. I will send down showers in season; there will be showers of blessing.
> Ezekiel 34:26

This last Scripture speaks of showers, a different type of rainfall. What is the definition of a shower? A shower is a fall of rain, especially heavy rain of short duration within a local area. To me, this scripture speaks of a special blessing granted in one particular area. It could be in the area of healing, finances, deliverance, or whatever the need is at that time. God's rain is falling all the time; however, there are times we get showers or bursts of rain for those special situations as God reveals His hand in our lives.

Prophetic Words Are Fulfilled in Their Season

> And he said, About this season according to the time of life, thou shalt embrace a son. And she said, Nay, my Lord, thou man of God, do not lie unto thine handmaiden. And the woman conceived, and bare a son at that season that Elisha had said unto her, according to the time of life.
> 2 Kings 4:16-17 (KJV)

> And now you will be silent and not able to speak until the day this happens, because you did not believe my words, which will come true at their proper time.
> Luke 1:20

When we are waiting for God to answer a request or to fill a need, we must remain patient. No matter how impossible God's promises may seem, what he said in His Word will come to pass.

What God promises, He will deliver, and God always delivers on time. We must have complete confidence that God will keep His promises. The fulfillment of the promises of God may not manifest the next day, month, or even year, but it will manifest "in the proper season and at the proper time." We must be assured in whom and what we believe and rest and wait for God's timing.

There Are Seasons of Heaviness and Seasons of Rejoicing

> "In this you greatly rejoice, though now for a little while you may have had to suffer grief in all kinds of trials."
>
> 1 Peter 1:6

All believers face trials, but we must accept trials as part of God's refining process. This process will cause impurities to rise to the surface so they can be removed. This will help us to grow into the kind of people God desires.

In any given season, storms may appear. What is a storm? A storm is a tempest, commotion, tumult; or assault on a fortified place. Storms can cause a disruption of our plans and our lives. We may be walking on cloud nine when the telephone rings, bearing unexpected news of a calamity or a loss. Even the best of seasons can be clouded by a storm. Storms come and storms go. They don't last forever. We must remember the sun will shine again. Today's turmoil often holds the sustenance and strength for the future. We must look for new growth that can come as a result of the storm.

Chapter VII

Season of Barrenness

We can also experience a season of barrenness. What does it mean to be barren? *Barren* means "incapable of producing, or not producing, offspring; sterile; not producing fruit, unfruitful; unprofitable, as an enterprise; not producing, lacking: *barren* of creative effort."

Different crops require a longer or shorter growing period in various seasons. No one would determine the worth of a fruit tree in the wintertime while it is barren and leafless. It is not expected to have fruit at this time. However, it is of concern if the fruit tree is in a season when it should be producing fruit. The same holds true for believers. There are times of barrenness and times of fruit production. The example below describes a tree that should have had fruit.

> Seeing a fig tree by the road, he went up to it
> but found nothing on it except leaves. Then he
> said to it, "May you never bear fruit again!"
> Immediately the tree withered.
> Matthew 21:19

Fig trees were a popular source of inexpensive food in Israel and required three years from the time they are planted until they can bear fruit. Each tree yields a great amount of fruit twice a year—in the late spring and in early autumn. When Jesus saw this tree, it was the spring fig season, when the leaves were beginning to bud. Figs normally grow as the leaves fill out, but this tree, though full of leaves, had no figs on it. The tree looked promising but offered no fruit.

Some people wonder why Jesus was so angry; after all, it was just a tree. We need to look at what the fig tree represents in order to apply this to our lives. Trees are a symbol of nations, individuals, or the church. In this instance, Jesus was directing His at anger at superficial religion, it appears promising but there is no performance. Let's apply this to an individual. We can relate this to a believer who is fruitful in appearance, but barren spiritually. If we are not putting faith to work in our lives then we are like the fig tree that has leaves but no fruit. This barrenness is not of God.

In this story, it seems Jesus knew the tree had all it needed to produce fruit, yet it did not. Jesus had a need; He was hungry and saw the tree from afar. The tree was at a stage where there should have been fruit. When He got close, He found no fruit. This is like the believer who attends church every Sunday and tells you of his good deeds, but when you get up close like the fruitless fig tree, you find it's all for show—there is no fruit. We must make sure we have faith working in our lives so that when others who have a need come to us, we will have fruit to give. The Word of God and faith will enable us grow unless we refuse to embrace it. On the outside we may say yes, amen, and hallelujah, and we may even look like we're on fire to others, but we can't fool God.

There are times of barrenness that are God-ordained. We see a picture of this with some of the notable women in the Bible:

Now Sarai was barren; she had no children.
Genesis 11:30

Then God said, Yes, but your wife Sarah will bear you a son...
Genesis 17:19

Isaac prayed to the Lord on behalf of his wife, because she was barren. The Lord answered his prayer, and his wife Rebekah became pregnant.
Genesis 25:21

When the: Lord saw that Leah was not loved, he opened her womb, but Rachel was barren.
Genesis 29:31

And God remembered Rachel, and God harkened to her, and opened her womb.

Genesis 30:22 (KJV)

But to Hannah he gave a double portion because he loved her, and the Lord had closed her womb... So in the course of time Hannah conceived and gave birth to a son.

1 Samuel 1:5, 20

And there was a certain man of Zorah, of the family of the Danites, whose name was Manoah; and his wife was barren, and bare not. And the angel of the LORD appeared unto the woman, and said unto her, Behold now, thou art barren, and bearest not: but thou shalt conceive, and bear a son.

Judges 13:2, 3 (KJV)

But they had no children, because Elizabeth was barren... But the angel said to him: Do not be afraid, Zechariah; your prayer has been heard. Your wife Elizabeth will bear a son...

Luke 1:7, 13

God shut their wombs so they could not produce fruit until the season He ordained. We must be patient and wait for God's timing or we might wind up with an Ishmael. Ishmael represents a fruit that was not produced of God. Abraham and Sarah are perfect examples of what happens when we try to produce our own fruit. Before their name change, Abram was promised a son with his wife Sarai. When he thought the promise would not be fulfilled, he followed Sarai's suggestion and took her Egyptian maid Hagar as a concubine in order to produce an heir. The son of that union was Ishmael. Isaac, the "child of promise," was finally born several years later. Things seemed all right for a while, but during the period when Isaac was being weaned, Sarah noted Ishmael teasing her son. She asked Abraham to send him and his mother away. So the two sons were separated, and there has been contention between their descendants to this day.

No matter what call we have on our lives or what promise is made to us by God, we must wait on Him. As hard as this might seem, if we don't wait and produce an Ishmael, we may regret knowing we missed God's best for the rest of our lives.

The principle of barrenness and fruitfulness relates to every individual whether married or single, young or old, male or female. Fruit produced in God's timing always brings joy.

Chapter VIII

God's Faithfulness

*F**aithful* is defined as "one who is true or trustworthy in the performance of duty, especially in the fulfillment of promises, obligations, and vows." Synonyms for faithfulness are devoted, firm, incorruptible, loyal, staunch, sure, true, trustworthy, trusty, and unwavering. When we think of faithfulness, a friend, relative, or spouse usually comes to mind. We can all find people in our lives who are faithful to us, accept us, and love us as we are. These special individuals are there for us even in those times when we are unlovable. Faithful people keep their promises—whether it's a promise of support or a vow—no matter how inconvenient it is for them.

If we can say these things about people, how much more can we say these same things about the God we serve? God's faithfulness surpasses human faithfulness. His love is absolute and His promises are irrevocable. He loves us in spite of our constant bent toward iniquity and sin. He keeps all the promises He has made to us, even when we break our promises to Him. God's faithfulness is perfect.

> O Lord, thou art my God; I will exalt thee, I will praise thy name; for thou hast done wonderful things; thy counsels of old are faithfulness and truth.
> Isaiah 25:1 (KJV)

Isaiah realized God completes His plans and promises, and because of this, Isaiah gave God honor and praise. When we are going through the various seasons, we must remember God also fulfills His promises to us. We, too, can acknowledge His goodness and faithfulness when we remember our previous answered prayers.

> Know therefore that the LORD thy God, he is God, the faithful God, which keepeth covenant and mercy with them that love him and keep his commandments to a thousand generations...
> Deuteronomy 7:9 (KJV)

It's good to know God can be counted on to faithfully carry out the promises made in any covenant or an agreement. There are a number of Scriptures in the psalms we can meditate on about God's faithfulness:

> Thy faithfulness is unto all generations…
> Psalm 119:90 a (KJV)

> All thy commandments are faithful.
> Psalm 119:86 a (KJV)

> Thy testimonies that thou hast commanded are righteous and very faithful.
> Psalm 119:138 (KJV)

It is a great comfort when we remember God is faithful throughout all generations and every season. We can rely on the fact that His promises cannot be outdated by the passing of time.

> But the Lord is faithful, who shall establish you, and keep you from evil.
> 2 Thessalonians 3:3 (KJV)

God is faithful to His promises and His purposes. We need to know what God has said and then we can remind Him we are standing on His promises. Our awareness of God's faithfulness will strengthen us.

> If we believe not, yet he abideth faithful: he cannot deny himself.
> 2 Timothy 2:13 (KJV)

Sometimes we struggle in a particular season and may we feel we have endured enough. We may even feel faithless at these times, but we must remember that God will not turn His back on us even if we turn our backs on Him.

> Wherefore let them that suffer according to the will of God commit the keeping of their souls to him in well doing, as unto a faithful Creator.
> 1 Peter 4:19 (KJV)

God is Creator and Master of the universe, and He has faithfully kept it going since its creation. Because we can see God's faithfulness demonstrated, we can count on Him to fulfill His promises to us. If God can oversee the universe, we can be assured He is able to see us through the seasons of life.

> It is of the Lord's mercies that we are not consumed, because his compassions fail not. They are new every morning: great is thy faithfulness.
> Lamentations 3:22, 23 (KJV)

We must trust in God's faithfulness day by day and be confident in His promises for our future.

> Your love, O Lord, reaches to the heavens, your faithfulness to the skies.
> Psalm 36:5

God is faithful, and no one can ever surpass the faithfulness of God.

Spring, summer and fall are generally not considered harsh seasons even when difficulties are encountered. But winter can be hash, and sometimes when a winter season is prolonged, we can come to the point where we feel as though God has forgotten us. If we are not careful, we can come to the conclusion that He cannot change our circumstances. This is a very dangerous thought process. We must cast down those imaginations; we must not spend one moment contemplating these kinds of thoughts. We must make every effort to keep our focus on God and His faithfulness and believe that He is in control. People who have no faith in God sometimes lose all hope and commit suicide because they believe there is no future. Christians are also susceptible to feelings of despair and hopelessness if they begin to doubt God's faithfulness. During these trying times, we should not doubt God. When we have questions, it's all right to ask God as shown in the following verses:

> And the children struggled together within her; and she said, If it be so, why am I thus? And she went to enquire of the LORD.
> Genesis 25:22 (KJV)

> When I tried to understand all this, it was oppressive to me; till I entered the sanctuary of God; then I understood their final destiny.
> Psalm 73:16-17

We must be careful that we do not murmur and complain. We must not allow ourselves to become loners and be isolated from others. The body of Christ, God's family, is here for a reason. We must continue to stay connected to the local church, where we can call on our fellow brothers and sisters to stand in agreement with us. We must be aware that these mind attacks are from the enemy and their intent is to make us break our focus and take us off the course God has planned for our lives. Satan does not want any of us to succeed and reach our full potential in God; he will do anything to hinder God's plan for us. But God is faithful. God has always been faithful because it is part of His character. We must understand God is not holding out on us or trying to hold something back from us, but in His faithfulness He is developing our natural gifts and talents while maturing us spiritually.

As we move from season to season, we must know that no matter what season we are in, God is faithful and is there for us. Our faith in His faithfulness will enable us to survive.

Chapter IX

Principles to Understanding the Seasons of God

There are principals to understanding the seasons of God, and there are attitudes and directions for any given season. Some of the areas we can explore are:

What Can We Expect and Experience in the Seasons of God?

1. We must fight battles. Although the battle is the Lord's, we must know how to protect ourselves.

   Put on the whole armour of God, that ye may be able to stand against the wiles of the devil. For we wrestle not against flesh and blood, but against principalities, against powers, against the rulers of the darkness of this world, against spiritual wickedness in high places. Wherefore take unto you the whole armour of God, that ye may be able to withstand in the evil day, and having done all, to stand.

Ephesians 6:11-13 (KJV)

2. We must not take shortcuts to bypass certain situations or circumstances because we can miss God's blessing.

Blessed is the man that endureth temptation: for when he is tried, he shall receive the crown of life, which the Lord hath promised to them that love him.

James 1:12 (KJV)

3. We must learn obedience. Jesus is our perfect example.

Though he were a Son, yet learned he obedience by the things which he suffered...

Hebrews 5:8 (KJV)

4. We must learn to depend and rely on God as is our source.

Not that we are sufficient of ourselves to think any thing as of ourselves; but our sufficiency is of God...

2 Corinthians 3:5 (KJV)

5. We must gain perspective, looking for God's viewpoint.

> For the ways of man are before the eyes of the LORD, and he pondereth all his goings.
> Proverbs 5:21 (KJV)

Some May Ask "Where is God?" We Must Know God Is Aware of Us in Every Season

1. God knows our every thought, word, and move.

> Thou knowest my downsitting and mine uprising, thou understandest my thought afar off.
> Psalm 139:2 (KJV)

2. God directs us no matter where we go.

> For I know the thoughts that I think toward you, saith the LORD, thoughts of peace, and not of evil, to give you an expected end.
> Jeremiah 29:11 (KJV)

3. God knows no hopeless or helpless situations.

> For with God nothing shall be impossible.
> Luke 1:37 (KJV)

4. God formed every complex detail of our bodies, minds, and spirits.

> Before I formed thee in the belly I knew thee…
> Jeremiah 1:5a (KJV)

5. God constantly thinks of us and is concerned with every detail of our lives.

> Therefore I say unto you, Take no thought for your life, what ye shall eat, or what ye shall drink; nor yet for your body, what ye shall put on. Is not the life more than meat, and the body than raiment?
> Matthew 6:25 (KJV)

6. God searches our hearts, and if we ask Him, He will purify our motives.

> For the word of God is quick, and powerful, and sharper than any twoedged sword, piercing even to the dividing asunder of soul and spirit, and of the joints and marrow, and is a discerner of the thoughts and intents of the heart.
> Hebrews 4:12 (KJV)

What Are Some Lessons We Can Learn in the Various Seasons?

1. It is our responsibility to recognize God's timing and not try to change it.

> Therefore judge nothing before the time, until the Lord come, who both will bring to light the hidden things of darkness, and will make manifest the counsels of the hearts: and then shall every man have praise of God.
> 1 Corinthians 4:5 (KJV)

2. It is our responsibility to accept and cooperate with God's timing.

   > Humble yourselves therefore under the mighty hand of God, that he may exalt you in due time...
   > 1 Peter 5:6 (KJV)

3. It is our responsibility to align ourselves with God's timing; it can make the difference between success and failure.

   > Faithful is he that calleth you, who also will do it.
   > 1 Thessalonians 5:24 (KJV)

4. It is our responsibility to know God has made everything appropriate in its time.

   > Which God will bring about in his own time...
   > 1 Timothy 6:15a

How Are We to View Seasons?

1. We must accept the fact we will be tested in each season and at each stage of growth.
2. We must use the time to be alone with God and become more intimate with Him.
3. We must remember the goal is to pass the test. God by His grace and mercy tells us through His Word how to pass the test. All we have to do is obey.
4. We must remember testing always precedes promotion or going to the next level.
5. We must realize self-promotion does not replace divine promotion.
6. We must realize godly promotion requires sacrifice.
7. We must remember not to compare our season to someone else's season.

Chapter X

Conclusion

Whatever season of life you are in right now, make full use of it! Even the dormant time of the winter season can become a special time for needed rest, quiet listening to God, and renewed study. Don't waste your time wishing you were someone else or that you were somewhere else or you were doing something else. We need to be at peace with God so we can discover, accept, and appreciate His perfect timing. We must keep in mind His promises may not be filled as soon as we expect or in the way we think is best. We must be careful of the danger when we begin to doubt or resent God's timing. This can lead to despair, rebellion, and moving ahead of God without His blessing.

God has a plan for each of us. Although we may face many problems that seem to contradict God's plan, these should not be barriers to believing in Him, but rather opportunities to discover that, without God, life's problems have no lasting solutions.

While God determines our season, our reaction to the season is our responsibility. God determines when a particular season comes; our responsibility is to tend to the soil of our heart and cultivate what has been planted in it. We can fill those times with reading, meditating, and studying the Word, which is the only way to benefit from these circumstances and situations. Yet we often resist the circumstances God has allowed in order to promote our growth. We must learn to be content in whatever season we find ourselves, knowing we are in the will of God.

> I am not saying this because I am in need, for I have learned to be content whatever the circumstances.
>
> Philippians 4:11

If we cooperate with God's seasons in our lives, we can experience great productivity and fruitfulness. But if we struggle against them, we will constantly be anxious, angry, and frustrated.

Another aspect about seasons we must understand is that our lives are not necessarily governed by only one season at a particular time. Different areas of our lives may be in different seasons. For example, have you been waiting for a promotion or a raise on your job? Are you waiting for that business to get off the ground? Do you feel you are in a "holding pattern"? This area of your life is in a winter season.

Are you starting to see the manifestation of that prophetic call on your life? Is your ministry coming into a clearer view, is your church settling down, are you starting to see a financial breakthrough? This area of your life is in a spring season.

Are you in any type of school or learning program and making an A on every exam or project this semester? Did you get that house you desired? Did you get that job or promotion you were waiting for? This area of your life is in a summer season.

Are you wondering what's happening with your relationships? Does it seem like you're growing apart from some friends? Do you find you're no longer interested in certain activities even though they are not bad? God may be trying to get you to reflect on where you are and where you are going. This area of your life is in a fall season. When we understand and realize this truth, our attitudes will change. We will trust the wisdom and love of God in every aspect of our lives.

Every season, from youth to old age, has its own responsibilities and rewards. Primary responsibilities change in various seasons, and as they do, new opportunities for growth become available. If we understand we are to be sensitive to the varying responsibilities of each season, we can reap the reward of a greater harvest in seasons to come.

Understanding the different seasons can relieve whatever pressure we may feel about our current circumstances and increase our faith and ability to obey God. God made us as we are, and He will use us as He planned. With each level of spiritual growth there will be new cycle of seasons. While we anticipate the fruit, we must understand the process.

I'd like to end with these words of encouragement: If we obey God, understand the seasons, embrace the rain, and endure the storms, then, as it says in Psalm 1:3, "...You will bring forth fruit in due season."

www.ingramcontent.com/pod-product-compliance
Ingram Content Group UK Ltd.
Pitfield, Milton Keynes, MK11 3LW, UK
UKHW041944230426
12048UKWH00008B/124